NATURE WATCH
SPIDERS

Barbara Taylor

Consultant: John Michaels

LORENZ BOOKS

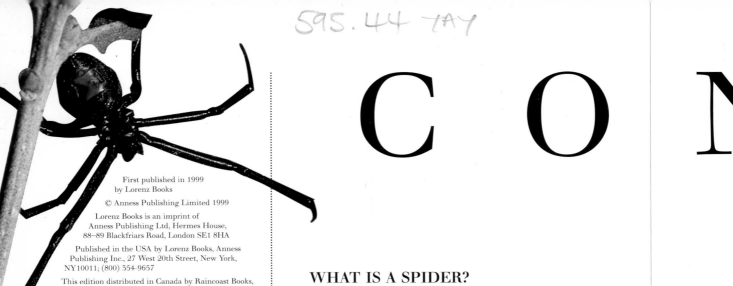

C O N

First published in 1999
by Lorenz Books

© Anness Publishing Limited 1999

Lorenz Books is an imprint of
Anness Publishing Ltd, Hermes House,
88–89 Blackfriars Road, London SE1 8HA

Published in the USA by Lorenz Books, Anness
Publishing Inc., 27 West 20th Street, New York,
NY10011; (800) 354-9657

This edition distributed in Canada by Raincoast Books,
8680 Cambie Street, Vancouver, British Columbia,
V6P 6M9

ISBN 1 85967 610 3

A CIP catalogue record for this book is available from
the British Library

Publisher: Joanna Lorenz
Managing Editor, Children's Books: Sue Grabham
Editor: Charlotte Hurdman
Designers: Traffika Publishing Ltd, Mirjana Nociar
Picture Researchers: Caroline Brooke-Johnson,
Kay Rowley
Special Photography: Kim Taylor
Illustrators: David Webb, Vanessa Card
Production Controller: Ann Childers
Reader: Penelope Goodare
With special thanks to Nicole Pearson

Printed and bound in Italy

10 9 8 7 6 5 4 3 2 1

The spiders used in this book are
all described using their common
English names first, followed by
their Latin names in *italic*. Where
a spider does not have a common
name, only its Latin name is given.

PICTURE CREDITS
b=bottom, t=top, c= centre, l= left, r= right
AKG: 16bl, 32br. Heather Angel: 21bl. Bridgeman Art
Library: 11b. BBC Natural History Unit/G Doré: 23b;
/Premaphotos: 43b; /Doug Wechsler: 12bl. Bruce
Coleman Ltd/Jane Burton: 17tr, 55t; /John Cancalosi: 9c;
/Gerald Cubitt:14t; /Adrian Davies: 48br; /A Dean: 51b;
/Jeremy Grayson: 23t, 51t; /Carol Hughes: 54t; /Janos
Jurka: 10br; /George McCarthy: 27t, 48bl; /Dieter &
Mary Plage: 53tr; /Andrew Purcell: 52b; /John Shaw:
6t; /Alan Stillwell: 13c, 16t, 48t, 50t, 51c; /Jan Taylor:
30t, 37br; /Kim Taylor: 15b, 26b, 28bl; /John Visser:
17tl, 35t; /Rod Williams: 7tr. Mary Evans Picture
Library: 5c, 21cr; /Arthur Rackham: 61cr. Michael and
Patricia Fodgen: 8bl, 32bl, 36t&b, 37t, 47b. FLPA: 17br,
55br; /Chris Mattison: 40c; /L Lee Rue: 33br; /Roger
Tidman: 54b; /Larry West: 31b, 43t, 53c; /Tony
Wharton: 55bc; /Terry Whittaker: 61t; /Roger
Wilmshurst: 59br. Fortean Picture Library: 58t.
Microscopix Photolibrary: 13b, 14b; /A Syred: 18c.
Natural Science Photos: 22b, 27b, 56t, 59tr. Nature
Photographers Ltd: 12br, 20bl, 27c, 47cr, 55bl. NHPA:
31tr, 42b, 56bl, 60t. Oxford Scientific Films: 25t, 46b,
43c, 61cl, 37bl. Papilio Photographic: 11t, 20br, 26t, 45tr,
47t, 53tl, 60b. Planet Earth Pictures/Gary Bell: 59bl;
/D. Maitland: 10t, 31tl; /Brian Kenney: 50br.
Ken Preston-Mafham/Premaphotos Wildlife: 6bl, 7b,
8br, 15tl & tr, 21cl, 23cl, 24b, 25c, 28t&br, 29b, 30b,
34l&r, 35bl&r, 38t&br, 39tr&b, 40t&b, 41t&c, 42t, 44t,bl
&br, 46t, 47cl, 49b, 52t, 53b, 57bl&br, 59tl. Dr Rod
Preston-Mafham/Premaphotos Wildlife: 6br, 16br,
17bl, 22t, 23cr, 32t, 38bl. Warren Photographic/Jane
Burton: 10bl, 19t, 41b, 45bl, 56br; /Jan Taylor: 5tl, 13tl,
39tl&c, 57t; /Kim Taylor: 5tr & b, 7c, 12t, 13tr, 20t, 21t,
29t, 33tl&tr, 45tl&br, 49c, 58b.

WHAT IS A SPIDER?

4 Introducing Spiders

6 Shapes and Sizes

8 Focus on Tarantulas

10 How Spiders Work

12 On the Move

14 Spider Eyes

SILK AND WEBS

16 Spinning Silk

18 Focus on Spinning a Web

20 Orb-Web Spiders

22 Hammocks, Sheets and Scaffolds

24 Sticky Traps

FOOD AND FEEDING

26 Catching Food

28 Focus on Hunting Jumping Spiders

30 Hidden Traps

32 Spider Venom

34 Fangs and Feeding

TENTS

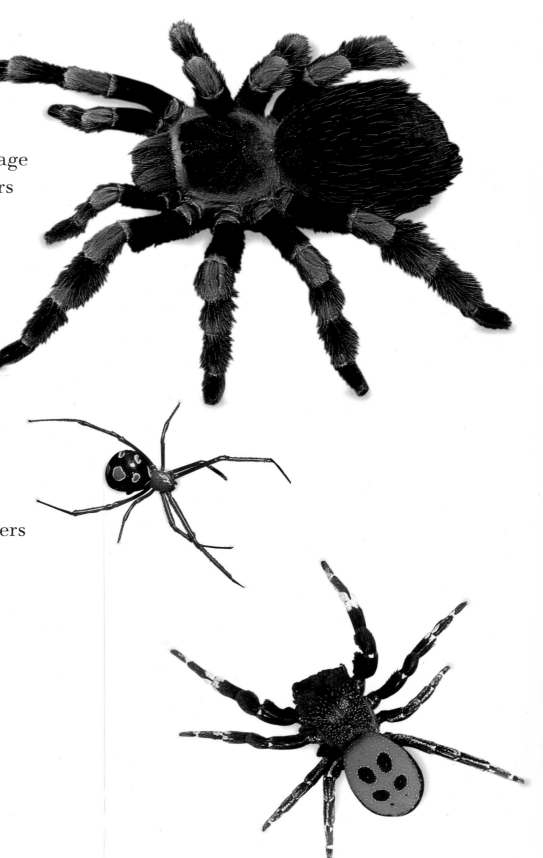

DEFENCE

36 Defence
38 Colour and Camouflage
40 Focus on Crab Spiders

LIFE CYCLES

42 Males and Females
44 Focus on Courtship
46 Spider Eggs
48 Spiderlings
50 Moulting

FACTS ABOUT SPIDERS

52 Spiders Everywhere
54 Focus on Water Spiders
56 Spider Families
58 Spider Relatives
60 Spiders and People
62 Glossary
64 Index

Introducing Spiders

Spiders are some of the most feared and least understood creatures in the animal world. These hairy hunters are famous for spinning silk and giving a poisonous bite. There are around 35,000 known species (kinds) of spider, with probably another 35,000 waiting to be discovered. Only about 30 species, however, are dangerous to people. Spiders are very useful to humans, because they eat insect pests and keep their numbers down. Spiders live nearly everywhere, from forests, deserts and grasslands, to caves, ships and in our homes. Some spin webs to catch their prey while others leap out from a hiding place or stalk their meals like tigers. There are even spiders that fish for their supper and one that lives in an air bubble underwater.

The front part of a spider is a joined head and chest called the cephalothorax. The body is covered by a tough skin called an exoskeleton. The shield-like plate on the top of the cephalothorax is called the carapace.

Spiders use palps for holding food and as feelers.

The chelicerae (jaws) are used to bite and crush prey. Each ends in a fang that injects poison.

A spider's eight hollow legs are joined to the cephalothorax.

The abdomen is the rear part of a spider. It is covered by soft, stretchy skin.

Silk is spun by organs called spinnerets at the back of the abdomen.

◄ **WHAT IS A SPIDER?**
Spiders are often confused with insects, but they belong to a completely different group. A spider has eight legs, but an insect has six. Its body has two parts while an insect's has three. Insects have antennae and many have wings, but spiders do not.

WEB WEAVERS ▶

About half of all spiders spin webs. They know how to do this by instinct from birth, without being taught. Many spiders build a new web each night. They build webs to catch prey. Spiders have a good sense of touch and can quickly tell if anything is caught in the web.

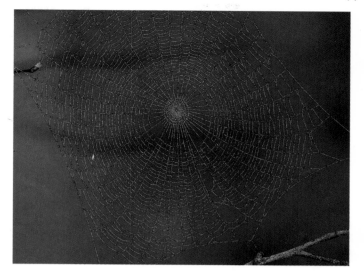

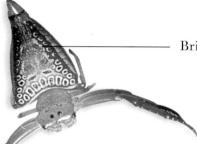

Bright colours help to conceal this spider among flowers.

▲ SPIDER SHAPES AND COLOURS

The triangular spider (*Arcys*) is named after its brightly coloured abdomen, which is shaped like a triangle. Its colour and shape help it to hide in wait for prey on leaves and flowers. Other spiders use bright colours to warn their enemies that they taste nasty.

Arachne's Tale
A Greek legend tells of Arachne, a girl who was very skilled at weaving. The goddess Athene challenged her to a contest, which Arachne won. The goddess became so cross Arachne killed herself. Athene was sorry and turned the girl into a spider so she could spin forever. Arachnid is the scientific name for spiders, named after Arachne.

◀ MALES AND FEMALES

Female spiders are usually bigger than the males and not so colourful, though this female *Nephila* spider is boldly marked. The male at the top of the picture is only one fifth of her size.

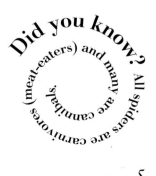

Did you know? All spiders are carnivores (meat-eaters) and many are cannibals.

Shapes and Sizes

Can you believe that there are spiders as big as frisbees or dinner plates? The world's biggest spider, the goliath tarantula of South America, is this big. Yet the smallest spider is only the size of a full stop. Apart from size, spiders also vary a great deal in their appearance. Many are an inconspicuous dull brown or grey while others are striking yellows, reds and oranges. Some spiders have short, wide bodies, while others are long, thin and skinny. There are round spiders, flat spiders and spiders with spines, warts and horns. A few spiders even look like ants, wasps or bird droppings!

▲ **FLOWER SPIDERS**
Using its shape and colour to hide on a flower, the flower spider (*Misumena vatia*) waits to ambush a visiting insect. This spider is one of a large family of crab spiders, so named because most of them have a similar shape to crabs.

Red-legged widow (*Latrodectus bishopi*)

Widow spiders often have bold black and red colouring.

Round, shiny abdomen.

Bristles on the back legs give the name comb-footed spider.

▲ **SPINY SPIDERS**
Some spiders have flat abdomens with sharp spines sticking out. This kite spider (*Gasteracantha*) has spines that look like horns. No one knows what these strange spines are for, but they may make it difficult for predators to hold or swallow the spider.

▲ **GRAPE SPIDERS**
Several kinds of widow spiders live in areas where grapes are grown. The females tend to have round abdomens, like a grape. Some of the most poisonous spiders belong to this group.

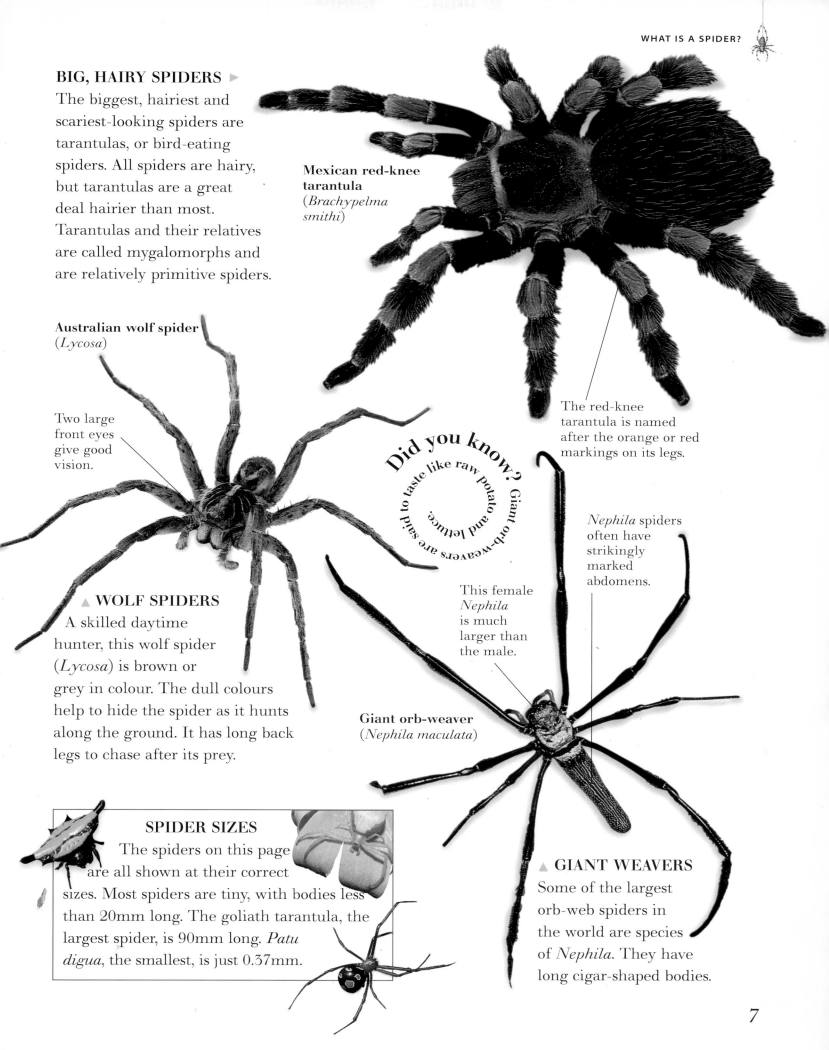

BIG, HAIRY SPIDERS ▶
The biggest, hairiest and
scariest-looking spiders are
tarantulas, or bird-eating
spiders. All spiders are hairy,
but tarantulas are a great
deal hairier than most.
Tarantulas and their relatives
are called mygalomorphs and
are relatively primitive spiders.

**Mexican red-knee
tarantula**
(*Brachypelma
smithi*)

Australian wolf spider
(*Lycosa*)

Two large
front eyes
give good
vision.

The red-knee
tarantula is named
after the orange or red
markings on its legs.

Did you know? Giant orb-weavers are said to taste like raw potato and lettuce.

Nephila spiders
often have
strikingly
marked
abdomens.

▲ **WOLF SPIDERS**
A skilled daytime
hunter, this wolf spider
(*Lycosa*) is brown or
grey in colour. The dull colours
help to hide the spider as it hunts
along the ground. It has long back
legs to chase after its prey.

This female
Nephila
is much
larger than
the male.

Giant orb-weaver
(*Nephila maculata*)

SPIDER SIZES
The spiders on this page
are all shown at their correct
sizes. Most spiders are tiny, with bodies less
than 20mm long. The goliath tarantula, the
largest spider, is 90mm long. *Patu
digua*, the smallest, is just 0.37mm.

▲ **GIANT WEAVERS**
Some of the largest
orb-web spiders in
the world are species
of *Nephila*. They have
long cigar-shaped bodies.

Giant salmon pink bird-eater (*Lassiodora parahybana*)

Focus on

The biggest, hairiest spiders are often called tarantulas, or bird-eating spiders. The large spiders we call tarantulas are all members of the family Theraphosidae. (The true tarantula, however, is a big wolf spider from southern Europe.) There are about 800 different species of tarantula living in warm or hot places all over the world. Many live in burrows, while some are tree-dwellers. Although they look scary, most tarantulas are shy, timid creatures and are harmless to people. A few have a very painful bite, but their poison is not deadly to humans.

WHICH NAME?

Known as tarantulas or bird-eating spiders in America and Europe, they are called baboon spiders in Africa. In Central America they are sometimes called horse spiders, as their bite was falsely believed to make a horse's hoof fall off.

Violet-black tarantula (*Pamphobeteus*)

Velvety, black carapace.

Abdomen covered in long brown hairs.

LIFE CYCLES

This red-knee tarantula (*Brachypelma smithi*) is shown guarding her eggs. Female tarantulas can live for more than 20 years and lay eggs at regular intervals when they become adults. After mating they may wait several months before laying their eggs.

FLOOR WALKERS

Violet-black tarantulas live on the floor of the Amazon rainforest. These spiders are active, impressive hunters. They do not build webs or burrows, but live out in the open.

Tarantulas

TARANTULA BODIES

Essentially a tarantula's body has the same parts and works in the same way as other spiders. Its eyesight is poor and it detects prey and danger with the many sensitive hairs that cover its body. Unlike other spiders, a tarantula can flick prickly hairs off its abdomen if it is attacked. On the ends of its legs are brushes of hairs that help it to climb on smooth surfaces. These hairs let some tarantulas walk on water.

Tiger rump doppelganger (*Cyclosternum fasciata*)

The back pair of legs is used to flick hairs off the abdomen at an enemy.

Many tarantulas use their strong legs to dig out burrows.

Tarantulas have eight tiny eyes, closely grouped together.

FEEDING TIME

Tarantulas usually feed on insects. This *Avicularia metallica* is eating a katydid, an insect like a grasshopper. Large tarantulas are able to take much larger prey, such as birds and snakes. They are slow eaters and may drag prey back to their burrows to feed.

FEARSOME FANGS

Tarantulas have large, hollow fangs that pump out venom as the spider bites. Most spiders bite with a sideways, pinching movement. Tarantulas bite straight down with great force, like a pickaxe.

Arizonan blond tarantula (*Aphonopelma chalcodes*)

How Spiders Work

From the outside, a spider's body is very different from ours. It has a hard outer skeleton, called an exoskeleton, and legs that have many joints. It has eyes and a mouth, but no ears, nose or tongue. Instead, it relies on a variety of hairs and bristles to touch, taste and hear things and it smells things with microscopic pores on its feet. Inside, a spider has many features common to other animals, such as blood, nerves, a brain and a digestive system. It also has special glands for spinning silk and for making and storing poison.

▲ SPIDER SKIN

A spider's exoskeleton protects its body like a suit of armour. It is made of a stiff material called chitin. A waxy layer helps to make it waterproof. The exoskeleton cannot stretch as the spider grows so must be shed from time to time. The old skin of a huntsman spider (*Isopeda*) is shown here.

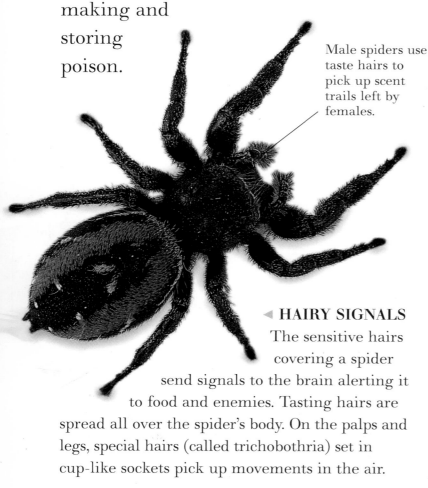

Male spiders use taste hairs to pick up scent trails left by females.

◄ HAIRY SIGNALS

The sensitive hairs covering a spider send signals to the brain alerting it to food and enemies. Tasting hairs are spread all over the spider's body. On the palps and legs, special hairs (called trichobothria) set in cup-like sockets pick up movements in the air.

▲ LEG SENSES

A green orb-weaver (*Araniella cucurbitina*) pounces on a fly. Spiders use special slits on their bodies to detect when an insect is trapped in their webs. These slits (called lyriform organs) pick up vibrations caused by a struggling insect. Nerve endings in the slits send signals to the spider's brain.

SPIDER POISON ▶

A spider is a delicate creature compared to the prey it catches. By using poison, a spider can kill its prey before the prey has a chance to harm its attacker. Spiders have two poison sacs, one for each fang. Bands of muscle around the sacs squeeze the poison down tubes in the fangs and out of a small opening in the end.

Poison gland linked to fang

Stomach muscle

Heart

Gut

Ovary (female reproductive organ)

Rectal sac

Pharynx muscle opens throat

Eyes

Chelicera (jaw)

Mouth

Brain

Sucking stomach

Folds in the book lung take in oxygen.

Trachea (breathing tube)

Silk glands

◀ **INSIDE A SPIDER**

The front part of a spider, the cephalothorax, contains the brain, poison glands, stomach and muscles. The abdomen contains the heart, lungs, breathing tubes, gut, waste disposal system, silk glands and reproductive organs. A spider's stomach works like a pump, stretching wide to pull in food that has been mashed to a soupy pulp. The heart pumps blood around the body.

Raiko and the Earth Spider
People have regarded spiders as dangerous, magical animals for thousands of years. This Japanese print from the 1830s shows the legendary warrior Yorimitsu (also known as Raiko) and his followers slaying the fearsome Earth Spider.

On the Move

Have you ever seen a spider scuttle swiftly away?
Spiders sometimes move quickly, but cannot keep
going for long. Their breathing system is not very
efficient so they soon run out of puff.

Spiders can walk, run, jump, climb and hang
upside down. Each spider's leg has seven sections.
The legs are powered by sets of muscles and blood
pressure. At the end of each leg are two or
three sharp claws for gripping surfaces.

Spiders that spin webs have a special claw to help
them hold on to their webs. Hunting spiders have
dense tufts of hair between the claws for gripping
smooth surfaces and for holding prey.

▲ **AERONAUT**
Many young or
small spiders drift
through the air on
strands of silk. Spiders
carried away on warm air
currents use this method
to find new places to live.

▲ **WATER WALKER**
The fishing spider (*Dolomedes fimbriatus*) is also called the raft
or swamp spider. It floats on the surface skin of water. Its long
legs spread its weight over the surface so it does not sink. Little
dips form in the stretchy skin of the water around each leg tip.

▲ **SAFETY LINE**
This garden spider (*Araneus*)
is climbing up a silk dragline.
Spiders drop down these lines
if they are disturbed. They
pay out the line as they go,
moving very quickly. As they
fall, spiders pull in their legs,
making them harder to see.

▲ SPIDER LEGS

Muscles in the legs of this trapdoor spider (*Aname*) bend the joints rather like we bend our knees. To stretch out the legs, however, the spider has to pump blood into them. If a spider is hurt and blood leaks out, it cannot escape from enemies.

▲ CHAMPION JUMPERS

Jumping spiders are champions of the long jump. They secure themselves with a safety line before they leap. Some species can leap more than 40 times the length of their own bodies.

▼ CLAWED FEET

Two toothed claws on the ends of a spider's feet enable it to grip surfaces as it walks. Web-building spiders have a third, middle claw that hooks over the silk lines of the web and holds the silk against barbed hairs. This allows the spider to grip the smooth, dry silk of its web without falling or slipping.

Scopulate pad

Toothed claw

Middle hook

Barbed hair

▲ HAIRY FEET

Many hunting spiders have dense tufts of short hairs called scopulae between the claws. The end of each hair is split into many tiny hairs a bit like a brush. These hairs pull up some of the moisture coating most surfaces, gluing the spider's leg down. Spiders with these feet can climb up smooth surfaces such as glass.

13

Spider Eyes

Spiders have poor eyesight and rely mainly on scents and vibrations to give them information about their surroundings. Even spiders with good eyesight, such as the jumping spiders, can see only up to 30cm away. Most spiders have eight eyes arranged in two or three rows. The eyes are pearly or dark and are usually protected by several bristles. Spider eyes are called ocelli and are of two types. Main eyes produce a focused image and help in pouncing on prey. Secondary eyes have light sensitive cells to pick up movement from a distance.

▲ **NO EYES**

This cave spider (*Spelungula cavernicola*) has no need for eyes, because there is no light in the cave for the spider to see. Like many animals that live in the dark it relies on other senses. It especially uses many sensitive hairs to find its way around, catch its prey and avoid enemies.

◄ **BIG EYES**

A spider's main eyes are always the middle pair of eyes in the front row. In most spiders the main eyes are small, but this jumping spider has very well developed main eyes, as this enlarged picture shows. They work rather like a telephoto lens on a camera. Inside, the large lens focuses light on to four layers of sensitive cells. The main eyes see clearly over a small area a few centimetres away and let the spider stalk and pounce when it gets close to its prey.

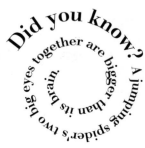

Did you know? A jumping spider's two big eyes together are bigger than its brain.

Eyes arranged in a compact group.

▲ HUNTSMAN SPIDER

The giant huntsman (*Holconia immanis*) is an agile, night-time hunter. Most hunting spiders have fairly large front eyes to help them find and pounce on prey. Secondary eyes help the hunters see in three dimensions over a wider area. They detect changes in light and dark.

▲ SHORT SIGHT

Spiders that spend much of their time under stones or in burrows usually have small eyes. This trapdoor spider (*Aname*) has eight tiny eyes in a close group. Spiders that catch their prey in webs also have very poor eyesight. These spiders rely much more on their sense of touch than their eyesight. They use their legs to test objects around them.

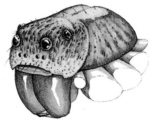

A large-eyed wolf spider (family Lycosidae).

The small eyes of an orb-weaver (family Araneidae).

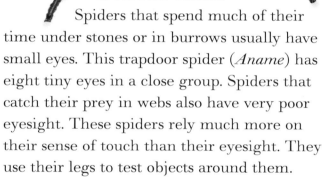

A six-eyed woodlouse spider (family Dysderidae).

A jumping spider (family Salticidae).

▲ EYES FOR HUNTING

The spiders with the best eyesight are active daylight hunters such as this jumping spider. A jumping spider's eight eyes are usually arranged in three rows with four in the front, two in the middle and two at the back. Lynx spiders and wolf spiders also have good eyesight.

▲ ALL KINDS OF EYES

The position and arrangement of a spider's eyes can be useful in telling which family it belongs to and how it catches food. A small number of spiders only have six eyes or fewer. Many male money spiders have eyes on top of little lobes or turrets sticking up from the head.

Spinning Silk

All spiders make silk. They pull the silk out of spinnerets on their abdomens, usually with their legs. The silk is a syrupy liquid when it first comes out, but pulling makes it harden. The more silk is pulled, the stronger it becomes. Some spider silk is stronger than steel wire of the same thickness. As well as being very strong, silk is incredibly thin, has more stretch than rubber and is stickier than sticky tape. Spiders make up to six different types of silk in different glands in the abdomen. Each type of silk is used for a different purpose, from making webs to wrapping prey. Female spiders produce a special silk to wrap up eggs.

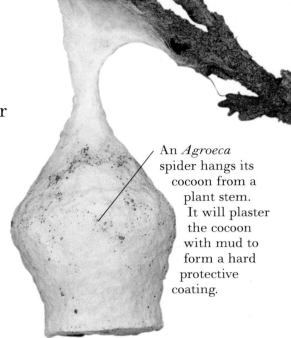

An *Agroeca* spider hangs its cocoon from a plant stem. It will plaster the cocoon with mud to form a hard protective coating.

▲ EGG PARCELS
Female spiders have an extra silk gland for making egg cases called cocoons. These protect the developing eggs.

The Industrious Spider
Spiders have been admired for their tireless spinning for centuries. This picture was painted by the Italian artist Veronese in the 1500s. He wanted to depict the virtues of the great city of Venice, whose wealth was based on trade. To represent hard work and industry he painted this figure of a woman holding up a spider in its web.

▲ A SILKEN RETREAT
Many spiders build silk shelters or nests. The tube-web spider (*Segestria florentina*) occupies a hole in the bark of a tree. Its tube-shaped retreat has a number of trip lines radiating out like the spokes of a wheel. If an insect trips over a line, the spider rushes out to grab a meal.

▲ STICKY SILK

Silk oozes out through a spider's spinnerets. Two or more kinds of silk can be spun at the same time. Orb-web spiders produce gummy silk to make their webs sticky.

SPINNERETS ▶

A spider's spinnerets have many fine tubes on the end. The smaller tubes, or spools, produce finer silk for wrapping prey. Larger tubes, called spigots, produce coarser strands for webs.

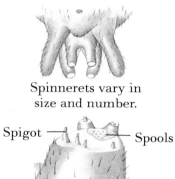

Spinnerets vary in size and number.

Spigot — Spools

Close up of a spinneret.

▲ FOOD PARCEL

A garden spider (*Araneus*) stops a grasshopper from escaping by wrapping it in silk. The prey is also paralysed by the spider's poisonous bite. Most spiders make silk for wrapping prey.

▲ COMBING OUT SILK

This lace-weaver (*Amaurobius*) is using its back legs to comb out a special silk. It has an extra spinning organ (the cribellum) in front of its spinnerets that produces loops of very fine silk.

▲ VELCRO SILK

The lacy webs made by cribellate spiders contain tiny loops, like velcro, that catch on the hairs and bristles of insect prey. Combined in bands with normal silk, the fluffy-looking cribellate silk stops insect prey from escaping.

Focus on

The orb-shaped (circular) web of an average garden spider (*Araneus*) is about 25cm across and uses 20 to 60m of silk. To build its web, the spider first attaches a line across a gap to form a bridge-line. The whole web will hang from this line. Suspended from the line, the spider makes a Y-shaped frame. From the hub (centre) of the Y, the spider spins a series of spoke-like threads. The spider then returns to the hub to spin a circular strengthening zone. From this zone, a temporary dry spiral of threads is laid out towards the edge of the web to hold the spokes in place. Starting from the outside, the spider now uses sticky silk to lay the final spiral. When the web is finished, the spider settles down to wait for a meal.

STICKY BEADS

As a spider spins the sticky spiral of its orb web it pulls the gummy coating into a series of beads, like a necklace. The dry spiral of silk is eaten as it is replaced. This spiral is no longer needed and the spider can recycle the nutrients it contains.

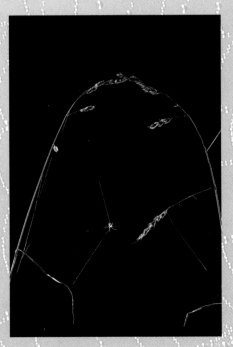

1 This garden spider is starting to spin a web. It has made a bridge-line from which it hangs down to pull the thread into a Y shape. The middle of the Y will be the centre of the web.

2 The spider then makes a framework, which looks like the spokes of a bicycle wheel. The spokes are called radii. From the centre, the spider now spins a dry spiral to hold the radii in place.

Spinning a Web

Spinning an orb web takes less than an hour. The spider either settles head downwards on the hub of the web, or hides in a retreat and keeps in touch through a signal thread held by the front legs.

3 Starting from the outside, the spider spins a sticky spiral. It does not go round in the same direction, but turns several times. A free zone between the sticky and dry spirals is left at the centre.

4 The completed web traps prey for long enough to give the spider time to work out its position. It feels how stretched the threads are in different parts of its web, then zooms in for the kill.

Orb-Web Spiders

The typical wheel-shaped orb web is spun by about 3,000 species of spider mostly in the family Araneidae. Some members of the Uloboridae also spin orb-shaped webs, using fluffy cribellar silk. Every orb-web spider will spin about 100 webs in its lifetime and has large silk glands. The orb web is a very clever way of trapping flying prey using the least amount of silk possible. This is important because spiders use up a lot of valuable body-building protein to spin silk. An orb web is almost invisible, yet it is very strong and elastic.

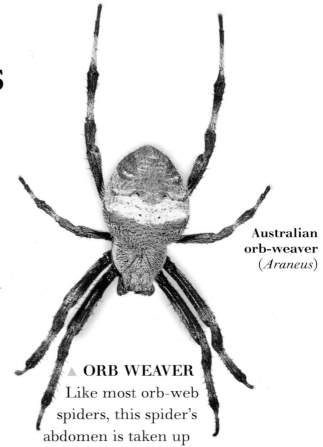

Australian orb-weaver (*Araneus*)

▲ **ORB WEAVER**
Like most orb-web spiders, this spider's abdomen is taken up by large silk glands. One gland makes the gummy silk to make its web sticky.

▲ **WEBS IN THE DEW**
Sticky beads on an orb web make it shimmer in the morning dew. The spiral threads of sticky capture silk stop flying or jumping insects from escaping.

◀ **SPINNING THE WEB**
An orb-web spider may spin a new web every night as fresh webs are the most efficient traps. The silk from old webs is usually eaten. The size of the web depends on the size of the spider — young spiders and smaller species spin smaller webs.

DECORATED WEBS ▶

Some orb weavers decorate their webs with stabilimenta (zigzags of silk). Young spiders tend to spin disc shapes, while adults build long lines. No one is sure what they are for — some may be for camouflage, but others are very obvious and may warn birds not to fly into the web.

▲ WAITING FOR A MEAL

As soon as a spider feels the vibrations made by prey struggling to escape, it moves in for the kill. It keeps its body clear of the sticky spirals, moving along the dry lines.

Madagascan orb-weaver (*Nephila inaurata*)

Did you know? One teaspoon of silk would be enough to make a million webs.

◀ GIANT NETS

Large, tropical *Nephila* spiders use tough yellow silk to build huge orb webs, some up to 2m across. These giant nets are incredibly strong and can catch small birds as prey.

The Spider and the King
In 1306, the king of Scotland Robert the Bruce was resting in a barn after defeat by the English. He watched a spider trying to spin its web. Six times the spider failed, but on the seventh attempt it succeeded. Inspired by this to fight on, Robert the Bruce finally defeated the English at Bannockburn in 1314.

Hammocks, Sheets and Scaffolds

Spiders build webs in many shapes and sizes apart from a typical orb web. Webs that look like sheets or hammocks are not sticky, but rely on a maze of criss-crossing threads to trap the prey. These are more suitable for trapping insects that walk or hop rather than those that fly. Most sheet-web spiders keep adding to their webs long after they are built. Scaffold webs have many dry, tangled threads, too, but they also have threads coated with sticky gum. Social spiders build huge communal webs that the spiders may hunt over in packs or alone.

▲ **HAMMOCK WEB**
A typical hammock web is supported by a maze of threads above and below the web. The silk is not sticky, but prey is tripped up by the threads to fall into the hammock below. The spider hangs upside down on the underside of the hammock waiting to grab prey from below and drag it through the web.

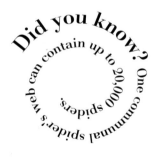

Did you know? One communal spider's web can contain up to 20,000 spiders.

◄ **TARANTULA WEB**
Large sheet webs are made by many tarantulas, trapdoor spiders and funnel-web spiders. This pink-toed tarantula (*Avicularia avicularia*) is sitting over the entrance of its tubular web. It mostly catches tree frogs and insects.

LADEN WITH DEW ▶

The hammock webs of money spiders (family Linyphiidae) show up well in the early morning dew. These webs are so named because the central sheet of the web sags like a hammock when it is laden with dew. Most hammock webs are only a few centimetres across, but some can be as big as dinner plates. There may be 50 or more hammock webs on just one gorse bush.

SHEET WEB ▶

The grass funnel-weaver (*Agelena labyrinthica*) builds a horizontal sheet web with a funnel-shaped shelter in one corner. The spider sits at the entrance to the funnel with its feet on the sheet waiting for an insect to get tangled in the maze of silk threads. The cobwebs made by house spiders (*Tegenaria*) in the corners of rooms are like this.

▲ SPIDER CITIES

Hundreds of dome-weavers (*Cyrtophora citricola*) build their webs together in what looks like a spider city. These huge webs almost cover trees. In the centre is a domed sheet like a trampoline. Although the spiders live closely together, each one defends its own web and may attack neighbours that come too close. Young spiders build their webs inside the framework of their mother's web.

◀ SCAFFOLD WEB

Comb-footed spiders (family Theridiidae) build three-dimensional trellises called scaffold webs. This scaffold is slung over a tall plant, but there are many different kinds. Many have a thimble-shaped retreat in which the spider eats its meal. Some threads are sticky, making it difficult for insects to escape.

Sticky Traps

A few spiders do not just build a web and wait for a meal to arrive. They go fishing for their food instead. The net-casting, or ogre-faced, spider throws a strong, stretchy net over its prey. It is also named the gladiator spider after the gladiators of ancient Rome. The bolas, or angling, spider is a very unusual orb-web spider that does not spin a web. It traps insects by swinging a thin line of silk with a sticky globule on the end, like a fishing hook on the end of a line. Spitting spiders are even more cunning. They fire poisonous glue to pin their prey to the ground.

Spider-Man
The bite of a radioactive spider gave the comic book character Spider-Man his special powers. He is very strong, with a keen sense that warns of danger, and he can cling to almost any surface. Web shooters on his wrists spray out sticky webs, which harden in the air. Spider-Man uses his unique powers to catch criminals.

◀ THE NET-CASTING SPIDER

At night, the stick-like net-casting spider (*Dinopis*) hangs from a twig holding a very stretchy, sticky silk net. As insects crawl or fly past the tiny net is stretched wide to trap them. The spider has huge eyes to help it to see at night, hence the name ogre-faced spider. It makes a new net each evening, eating the old one even if it is unused.

The net-casting spider hangs upside down, holding its elastic net in its front four legs. The legs are kept drawn in close to the body while the spider waits.

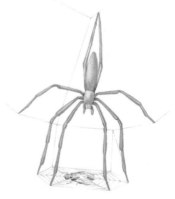

When an insect, such as an ant, scurries past, the spider opens the net and quickly drops down. It scoops up its meal then springs back up.

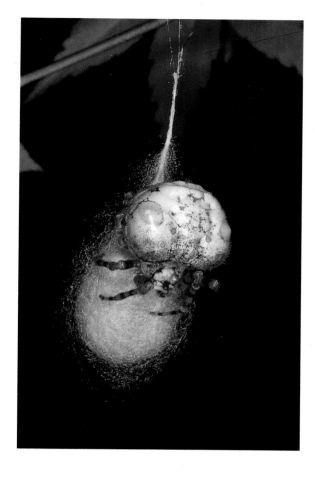

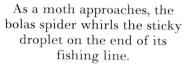

As a moth approaches, the bolas spider whirls the sticky droplet on the end of its fishing line.

A moth is stuck fast to the sticky drop and is trapped. The spider pulls in the line and starts to feed.

◀ FISHING FOR FOOD

This female bolas spider (*Mastophora*) is making a large egg case. Bolas spiders catch moths by using sticky balls on the end of a silk line. The spiders are named after the bolas (a strong cord connecting three balls) used by South American cowboys to trip up cattle. The spider produces a scent just like that made by female moths to draw male moths to its fishing line.

SPITTING SPIDER ▶

This female spitting spider (*Scytodes*) is carrying a ball of eggs in her jaws. Spitting spiders produce glue as well as poison inside the poison glands in the front half of the body. When the spider is very close to its prey, it squirts out two lines of gummy poison from its fangs to pin down the victim. It then gives its prey a poisonous bite before tearing it free of the glue and eating its meal.

The spitting spider's fangs move from side to side as it squirts out its sticky poison. This imprisons the victim under two zigzag strands of quick-setting glue.

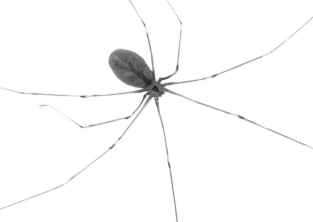

◀ SIMPLE NETS

The daddy-longlegs spider (*Pholcus*) spins a flimsy scaffold web that is almost invisible. When an insect, or another spider, gets tangled up in its web, the daddy-longlegs throws strands of fresh silk over its prey. It can do this from a distance because of its long legs. Once the victim is helpless, the spider moves in for the feast.

25

Catching Food

Only about half of all spiders spin webs to catch prey. Of the other half, some hide and surprise their victims with a sneak attack — crab spiders do this very well. Others, such as trapdoor spiders, set traps as well as ambushing prey. Many spiders, such as jumping spiders, are agile, fast-moving hunters that stalk their prey. Spiders are not usually very fussy about what they eat. Insects, such as grasshoppers, beetles, ants and bees are their main food, but some eat fish, while bigger spiders may catch mice and birds. Many spiders eat other spiders.

▲ SILK TRAPS

Orb webs are designed to catch insects up to about the size of the spiders that made them. This orb-web spider is eating a crane-fly. The prey has been bitten and wrapped in silk, then cut free from the web and carried away to be eaten. Some insects, such as moths, manage to escape from webs. Smaller spiders tend to free large insects from their webs before they do too much damage.

The empty shell of a partly eaten fly.

Dead flies wrapped in silk are left hanging for eating later.

◀ DAISY WEB

In the centre of this ox-eye daisy sits a green orb-web spider (*Araniella cucurbitina*). It has built its web over the middle of the daisy. Small flies, attracted to the innocent-looking flower, are trapped in the web. They end up as food for the spider who kills them, then crushes them to a pulp before sucking up a meal.

WATER HUNTER ▶

This fishing spider (*Dolomedes*) has caught a blue damselfly. It lives in swamps and pools where it sits on the leaves of water plants. It spreads its legs on the water's surface to detect ripples from insects that fall into the water, then rushes out to grab them. Fish swimming in the water below are also caught by this hunting spider. The spider may even dabble its legs in the water to attract small fish towards its waiting fangs.

◀ HAIRY HUNTER

Tarantulas are also called bird-eating spiders and they really do eat birds, although this one has caught a mouse. They also eat lizards, frogs and even small poisonous snakes. But most of the time, tarantulas feed on insects. They hunt at night, finding their prey by scent or by picking up vibrations with their sensitive hairs. After a quick sprint and a bite from powerful jaws, the spider can tuck into its meal. It may take as long as a day to suck the body of a snake dry.

ATHLETIC HUNTER ▶

Lynx spiders hunt their prey on plants. They sometimes jump from leaf to leaf after their prey, but at other times they sit and wait. The green lynx spider (*Peucetia*) is an athletic hunter with long spiny legs that enable it to leap easily from stem to stem. It often eats other spiders and is even a cannibal, eating members of its own species. This one has caught a termite.

27

Focus on Hunting

With bright, shiny colours like a peacock, large curious eyes like a cat and the agility to jump like a monkey, little jumping spiders are one of the most extraordinary spider families. Belonging to the family Salticidae, there are about 4,000 different kinds, many of which live in warmer parts of the world. Most jumping spiders are always on the prowl, darting jerkily along, peering all around for a possible meal. They can see in colour and form clear images of their prey. They stalk their prey rather like a cat stalks a mouse, crouching before the final pounce. Jumping spiders will turn their tiny heads to peer closely at a human face looking at them.

SIGN LANGUAGE
A male jumping spider's front legs are longer and thicker than a female's. He uses them in courtship dances, waving them about like sign language.

PREPARING TO LEAP
Before it jumps, the spider fixes itself firmly to a surface with a silk safety line. Then it leaps on to its target, pushing off with the four back legs. The Australian flying spider (*Satis volans*) also has wing-like flaps so it can glide during leaps.

STURDY LEGS
This female heavy jumper (*Hyllus giganteus*) is feeding on a leaf-hopper. A jumping spider's legs do not seem to be specially adapted for jumping. Their small size (less than 15mm long) and light weight probably help them to make amazing leaps.

Jumping Spiders

THE BIG LEAP

A jumping spider's strong front legs are often raised before a jump, stretched forwards in the air, and used to hold the prey when the spider lands. Scopulae (hairy tufts) on the feet help jumping spiders grip smooth and vertical surfaces. They can even leap away from a vertical surface to seize a flying insect.

JUMPING CANNIBALS

Jumping spiders will feed on their own relatives. This female two-striped jumping spider (*Telamonia dimidiata*) is feeding on another species of jumping spider. Some unusual *Portia* jumping spiders vibrate the webs of orb-weaving spiders, like an insect struggling to escape. When the orb-weaver comes out to investigate, the *Portia* spider pounces.

Hidden Traps

Some spiders do not go hunting for food. They prefer to lurk inside underground burrows or tubes of silk and wait for a meal to come by. Silk threads around the entrance to the burrow trip up passing insects and other small creatures. Inside the burrow, the spider feels the tug on its trip lines, giving it time to rush out and pounce on the prey before it can escape. Patient, lie-in-wait spiders include trapdoor spiders, which have special spines on their fangs to rake away the soil as they dig. The burrows also shelter spiders from the weather and help them to avoid enemies.

▲ SILK DOORS

The lid of a trapdoor spider's burrow is made of silk and soil with a silk hinge along one side. The door usually fits tightly into the burrow opening and may be camouflaged with sticks, leaves and moss. Where flooding occurs, walls or turrets are built around the entrance to keep out the water.

The spider waits for an insect to land on its tube-like web.

The spider spears the insect with its sharp jaws.

▲ A SILKEN TUBE

This purse-web spider (*Atypus affinis*) is shown outside its burrow. It usually lives inside a tubular purse of densely woven silk. The tube is about 45cm long and about the thickness of a finger. Part of it sticks up above the ground or from a tree trunk, and is well camouflaged with debris.

▲ INSIDE A PURSE-WEB

Inside its silken purse the spider waits for any insect to walk over the tube. It spears the insect through the tube with its sharp jaws and drags the prey inside.

▲ FUNNEL-WEB SPIDERS

The Sydney funnel-web (*Atrax robustus*) is one of the deadliest spiders in the world. It lives in an underground burrow lined with silk. From the mouth of the burrow is a funnel that can be up to 1m across. Trip wires leading from the funnel warn the spider that prey is coming. The spider can dig its own burrow with its fangs, but prefers to use existing holes and cracks. Funnel-web spiders eat mainly beetles, large insects, snails and small mammals.

▲ TRIP WIRES

The giant trapdoor spider (*Liphistius*) may place silken trip lines around the entrance to its burrow to detect the movements of a passing meal. If it does not have trip lines, the spider relies on detecting the vibrations of prey through the ground. If it senses a meal is nearby, the spider rushes out of its burrow to grab the prey in its jaws.

Did you know? Trapdoor spiders may live for up to 20 years in their burrows.

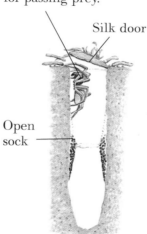

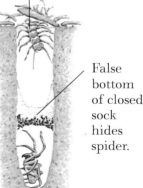

Spider looking out for passing prey.

Silk door

Centipede enters spider's burrow.

Open sock

False bottom of closed sock hides spider.

▲ ODD SPIDER OUT

Some unusual wolf spiders live in underground burrows. This tiger wolf spider (*Lycosa aspersa*) has dug out the soil with its fangs and lined the walls of its burrow with silk. To camouflage the entrance it has built a wall of twigs and litter.

▲ ALL KINDS OF TRAPS

Trapdoor spiders' burrows range from simple tubes to elaborate lairs with hidden doors and escape tunnels. The burrow of *Anidiops villosus* has a collapsible sock. The spider pulls it down to form a false bottom, hiding it from predators.

Spider Venom

Nearly all spiders use poison to kill or paralyse their prey and for defence. (Only spiders in the family Uloboridae have no poison glands.) Spider poison is called venom. It is injected into prey through fangs. There are two main kinds of venom that can have serious effects. Most dangerous spiders, such as widow spiders (*Lactrodectus*), produce nerve poison to paralyse victims quickly. The other kind of venom works more slowly, destroying tissues and causing ulcers and gangrene. It is made by the recluse spiders (*Loxosceles*). Spider venom is intended to kill insects and small prey – only about 30 spider species are dangerous to people.

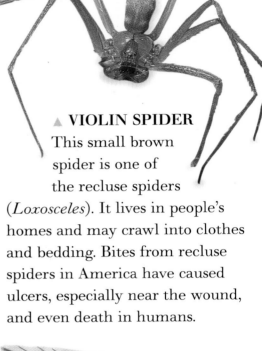

▲ **VIOLIN SPIDER**
This small brown spider is one of the recluse spiders (*Loxosceles*). It lives in people's homes and may crawl into clothes and bedding. Bites from recluse spiders in America have caused ulcers, especially near the wound, and even death in humans.

▲ **WANDERING SPIDER**
The Brazilian wandering spider (*Phoneutria fera*) is a large hunting spider that produces one of the most toxic of all spider venoms. If disturbed it raises its front legs to expose its threatening jaws. It has the largest venom glands of any spider (up to 10mm long), which hold enough venom to kill 225 mice. Several people have died from this spider's bite.

The Spider Dance
In the Middle Ages people from Taranto in southern Italy called the large wolf spider Lycosa narbonensis *the tarantula. They believed the venom of this spider's bite could only be flushed from the body by doing the tarantella, a lively dance. However,* Lycosa's *bite is not serious. An epidemic of spider bites at the time was probably caused by the malmignatte spider* (Latrodectus tredecimguttatus).

▲ THE QUICK KILL

Crab spiders do not spin webs so they need to kill their prey quickly. They usually inject their venom into the main nerve cords in the neck where the poison will get to work most rapidly. They are able to kill insects much larger than themselves, such as bees.

WIDOW SPIDER ▶

The Australian red-back spider (*Latrodectus hasselti*) is one of the most deadly widow spiders. Widow spiders are named after the female's habit of eating the male after mating. Only female widow spiders are dangerous to people – the much smaller male's fangs are too tiny to penetrate human skin.

Did you know? A black widow's venom is 15 times more poisonous than a rattlesnake's.

▲ GENTLE GIANT

Tarantulas look very dangerous and have huge fangs, but at worst their bite is no more painful than a wasp sting. They have small venom glands and are unlikely to bite unless handled roughly. They use venom to digest their prey.

▲ BLACK WIDOW

The American black widow (*Latrodectus mactans*) is another spider with venom powerful enough to kill a person (although medicines can now prevent this happening). These shy spiders hide away if disturbed, but like to live near people. Of the main ingredients in their venom, one knocks out insects and another paralyses mammals and birds by destroying their nervous systems.

Fangs and Feeding

A spider's sharp, pointed fangs are part of its jaws. Each fang is like a curved, hollow needle. It is joined to a basal segment, which joins on to the spider's body just in front of the mouth. The fangs may be used for digging burrows and carrying eggs, but are mainly used for injecting venom and for defence. Venom passes through a tiny hole near the end of each fang. Although the fangs are not very long, the venom they deliver makes them into powerful weapons. Once prey is caught, a spider uses its jaws, palps and digestive juices to mash up its prey into a soggy, soupy lump. This is because a spider's mouth is too small for solid food. Then the spider sucks up the liquid food into its stomach. Its abdomen swells as the food is swallowed, so a spider looks fatter after a meal.

FROG SOUP ▶

Spiders sometimes have to turn quite large items of food into pulp before they can suck up a meal. This rusty wandering spider (*Cupiennius getazi*) is turning a tree frog over and over to mash it up in its jaws. It finds the frogs by using the slit organs on its feet to detect the mating calls they make.

▲ **A SOGGY MEAL**

This garden spider (*Araneus diadematus*) has turned her prey into a soupy meal. The basal segments of the jaws often have jagged edges to help the spider tear and mash up its prey. Smaller jaws, called maxillae, on either side of the mouth are also used to turn prey into a liquid pulp.

Did you know? A Sydney funnel-web's fangs are strong enough to pierce bone.

34

DAGGER FANGS ▶

This tarantula's dagger-like fangs have pierced through the skin of a baby field mouse to inject venom into its body. The venom glands of tarantulas and trapdoor spiders are all inside the basal segments of the jaws. They do not extend into the head as in most other spiders. Tarantula venom can kill a small animal and causes burning and swelling in a person.

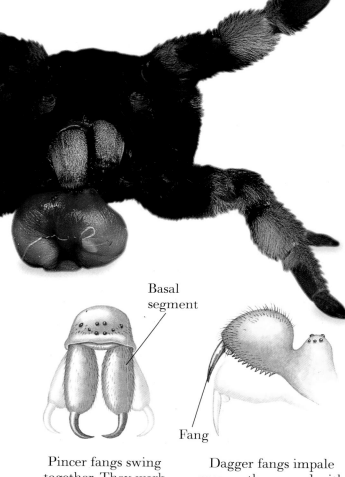

HOW FANGS WORK ▶

In most spiders, the fangs face each other and close together like pincers or pliers. In mygalomorph spiders (tarantulas and trapdoor spiders), however, the fangs stab downwards like two daggers. The spider has to raise its front end to strike forwards and down on to its prey. Prey needs to be on a firm surface such as the ground for these jaws to work.

Basal segment

Fang

Pincer fangs swing together. They work well on webs and leaves.

Dagger fangs impale prey on the ground with a downwards action.

▲ FANGS FOR DEFENCE

An Australian trapdoor spider (*Aname*) tries to make itself look as frightening as possible if it is threatened. It tilts back its body and raises its front legs so that its long poisonous fangs are easy to see. It adopts this aggressive pose to warn an enemy to leave it alone.

▲ PINCER FANGS

The lobed argiope spider (*Argiope lobata*) has fangs that work like pincers. It catches large insects in its orb web and wraps them in silk before biting them. As in most spiders, the venom glands go well back inside the head.

35

Defence

Spiders are small, with juicy bodies that make a tasty meal for many predators. To avoid their enemies, such as other spiders, hunting wasps, lizards and frogs, many spiders hide away. Trapdoor spiders hide in well-concealed burrows. Other spiders hide themselves by being beautifully camouflaged to blend in with their surroundings. In complete contrast, some spiders copy the bright colours of dangerous insects, such as wasps. This tricks enemies into leaving the spider alone. Spiders will even pretend to be dead, since predators prefer to eat live prey.

The spider raises its legs high up and waves them about to look more aggressive.

▼ THREATENING DISPLAY

The golden wheel spider (*Carparachne aureoflava*) lives on the sand dunes of the Namib Desert, southern Africa. Its gold colour blends in well with its surroundings. If caught out in the open, however, the spider rears up to make itself look larger and more frightening to enemies.

By raising its abdomen high into the air, the spider makes itself appear larger.

Standing on tiptoe also helps to make it look larger.

ESCAPE WHEEL ▶

If the golden wheel spider's threatening display does not deter an enemy, it has another, remarkable way of escaping. The spider throws itself sideways, pulls in its legs and rolls itself into a ball. It then cartwheels rapidly away down the dunes.

HUNTING WASP ▶

This hunting wasp has just paralysed a spider with its sting. Most wasps that hunt spiders are solitary pompilid wasps. A wasp will attack spiders as large or larger than itself. First it stings the spider to paralyse it. Then it drags the spider off to a burrow, lays an egg on its body and buries the spider alive. When the egg hatches out, the wasp grub feeds on the spider meat. The spider provides a living larder for the grub as it grows.

▲ SPIDER ENEMIES

A hungry lizard crunches up a tasty spider meal. Many animals eat spiders, including frogs, toads, mice, shrews, monkeys, bandicoots and possums. Birds are not usually a threat, because most spiders are active at night when few birds are about. The most common enemies of spiders, however, are probably the smaller animals without backbones. These include other spiders, hunting wasps, assassin bugs, scorpions and centipedes.

Did you know? Daddy-long-legs spiders jump up and down to scare away enemies.

FIGHTING ON YOUR BACK ▶

This venomous spider throws itself on its back to display its warning colours when it is attacked. Colours such as yellow, orange, red and black are warning signals, saying "I am poisonous, leave me alone". Other active defence tactics include showing off the fangs and squirting liquid or venom at an attacker.

Bold markings on the underside warn enemies to leave this spider alone.

Colour and Camouflage

Is it a leaf, a twig or a piece of bark? Is it a bird dropping? No, it is a spider! Many spiders have bodies that are coloured and shaped just like objects in their surroundings. They are so well camouflaged that they are very hard to see, especially when they keep still. This allows the spider to sit out in the open where it can more easily catch food, yet remain invisible to its enemies and prey. A few spiders, such as crab spiders and some jumping spiders, can even change colour to match different backgrounds. It takes some time for the spider to do this, however. Brightly coloured spiders often taste nasty. These eye-catching colours warn enemies to leave them alone.

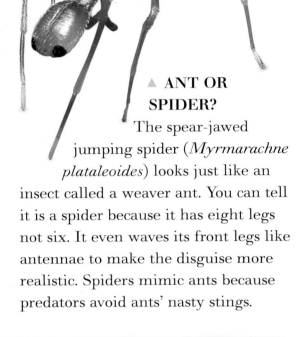

▲ ANT OR SPIDER?

The spear-jawed jumping spider (*Myrmarachne plataleoides*) looks just like an insect called a weaver ant. You can tell it is a spider because it has eight legs not six. It even waves its front legs like antennae to make the disguise more realistic. Spiders mimic ants because predators avoid ants' nasty stings.

▲ SAND SPIDER

When spiders are the same colour or pattern as their background they can be hard to spot. The wolf spider *Arctosa perita* lives on sand or gravel. Its speckled colouring breaks up the outline of its body so it is hard to see. Until it moves, the spider is almost invisible.

▲ LOOKING LIKE A FLOWER

With their colours matching all or part of a flower, many crab spiders lurk on the surface of plants waiting to catch insects. This is the seven-spined crab spider (*Epicadus heterogaster*). The fleshy lobes on its abdomen imitate the host plant's white, orchid-like flowers.

▲ LEAF LOOK-ALIKE

Spiders like this *Augusta glyphica* have lumpy or wrinkled abdomens. With their legs drawn up, they look just like a piece of dead leaf.

▲ BIRD DROPPING

Looking like a bird dropping is a very useful disguise for many spiders. Enemies are not likely to eat droppings and some insects are attracted to feed on the salts they contain. A few spiders even release a scent similar to bird droppings.

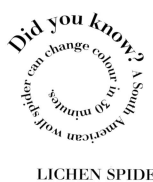

Did you know? A South American wolf spider can change colour in 30 minutes.

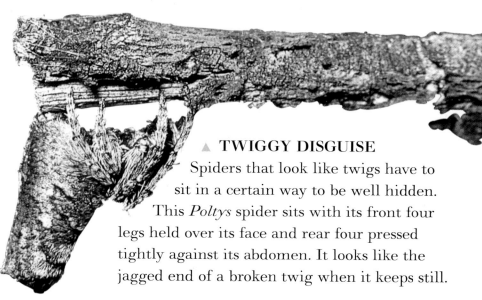

▲ TWIGGY DISGUISE

Spiders that look like twigs have to sit in a certain way to be well hidden. This *Poltys* spider sits with its front four legs held over its face and rear four pressed tightly against its abdomen. It looks like the jagged end of a broken twig when it keeps still.

LICHEN SPIDER ▶

The lichen huntsman (*Pandercetes gracilis*) from the rainforests of Australia and New Guinea spends all day pressed close to the bark of a tree. The spider's mottled colours match the colours of the lichens on the tree. Short hairs also give the colours a matt finish. All along its legs and the sides of its body, fringes of hair stop the spider casting a shadow.

BODY PARTS

Crab spiders are usually not very hairy and many, like this heather spider (*Thomisus onustus*), are brightly coloured. They often have wart-like lumps and bumps on their bodies, especially the females. The front pairs of legs are adapted for grasping prey.

COLOUR CHANGE

Female flower spiders (*Misumena vatia*) can change colour. A yellow pigment is moved from the intestines (gut) to the outer layer of the body to turn yellow and back again to turn white. It takes up to two days for the spider to complete the change.

Focus on

With broad, flat bodies and sideways scuttling movements like crabs, the members of the family Thomisidae are called crab spiders. There are about 3,000 species living all over the world. Crab spiders do not usually build webs. They often lie in wait for their prey on flowers, leaves, tree trunks or on the ground. Most are small (less than 20mm long) and rely on stealth and strong venom to catch prey. Males are often half the size of the females and their colours can be quite different.

BIG EATERS

Crab spiders can kill larger prey than themselves. This gold leaf crab spider (*Synema globosum*) has caught a honeybee. Its venom is powerful, quickly paralysing the bee. This avoids a long struggle, which might damage the spider and draw the attention of enemies.

Crab Spiders

SIX-SPOT CRAB SPIDER

The unusual six-spot crab spider (*Platythomisus sexmaculatus*) has very striking markings. These might be warning colours, but very little is known about this spider. No one has ever seen a male six-spot crab spider. The female, shown here, is about 15mm long in real life.

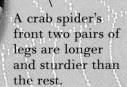

Eight small eyes give quite good vision.

A crab spider's front two pairs of legs are longer and sturdier than the rest.

FEEDING TIME

This common crab spider (*Xysticus cristatus*) is eating a dance fly. Crab spiders do not store prey like many other spiders. They can only deal with one meal at a time. Insects can pass close by a feeding crab spider unnoticed. A crab spider's jaws have no teeth and cannot mash up its prey. Instead, fangs inject digestive juices that break down the prey's insides. The spider sucks up its liquid meal, leaving a dry, empty husk behind.

THE AMBUSH

This flower spider (*Misumena vatia*) has sat on a daisy for several days. It hardly moved as it waited to ambush an insect, such as a bee. The two rear pairs of legs anchored the spider firmly on to the flower. The two front pairs of legs, armed with bristles, grabbed the bee like pincers.

Males and Females

Most spiders spend much of their life alone, only coming together to mate. Females often look different from males. The female is usually larger because she needs to carry a lot of eggs inside her body. She also has extra glands to make a silk covering for her eggs. The female may even guard the eggs and young spiderlings after they hatch. She is also usually a drab colour to help hide her and her young from enemies. The male, on the other hand, takes no part in looking after his family after mating. He is usually smaller and sometimes more colourful. Males often have longer legs to help search for a mate.

▲ **SPERM WEB**
This male garden spider (*Araneus diadematus*) is filling his palps with sperm before searching for a mate. He has made a small web and squirted some sperm on to it. He sucks up the sperm into the swollen tip of each palp.

▲ **MALE MEALS?**
The much larger female black widow spider (*Latrodectus mactans*) sometimes eats the smaller, brown male after mating. Other female spiders occasionally do this, too. The most dangerous time for many males, however, is before mating. If the female is not ready to mate or does not recognize the male's signals, she may eat the male before he has a chance to mate.

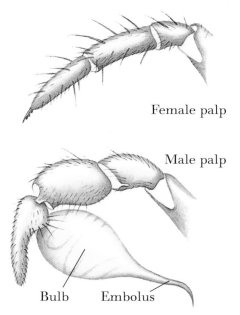

Female palp

Male palp

Bulb   Embolus

▲ **DIFFERENT PALPS**
Males have larger palps than females. The embolus on the tip of a male's palp is used to suck up sperm into the bulb. It pumps sperm out into the female's body during mating.

42

◀ EGG CARRIER

This female *Sosippus mimus* is spinning a silk cocoon to protect her eggs. The number of eggs laid by a female spider usually depends on her size. Some tiny spiders, such as *Atrophonysia intertidalis*, lay only one egg, while large *Nephila* spiders lay 1,000 or more. A spider's abdomen has a fairly thin covering, so it can stretch a great deal when a female has many eggs developing inside.

SPOT THE DIFFERENCE ▶

This male and female ladybird spider (*Eresus niger*) show very clearly the differences between some male and female spiders. Their difference in size varies a great deal, but adult females can be over three times the size of males. The female is well camouflaged in a velvety blue-black skin, while the male looks like a brightly-coloured ladybird. He will run across open ground in search of a mate in spring. She usually hides away under stones.

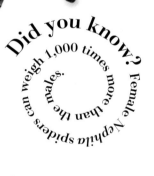

Female ladybird spider (maximum body length up to 35mm)

Male ladybird spider (maximum body length up to 10mm)

Did you know? Female *Nephila* spiders can weigh 1,000 times more than the males.

LITTLE AND LARGE ▶

A tiny male giant orb-weaver (*Nephila maculata*) mates with a huge female. They look so different it is hard to believe that they are the same species. The very small size of the male helps him to avoid being eaten by the female, since he is smaller than her usual prey. The female has two openings on her underside to receive sperm from the male's palps.

43

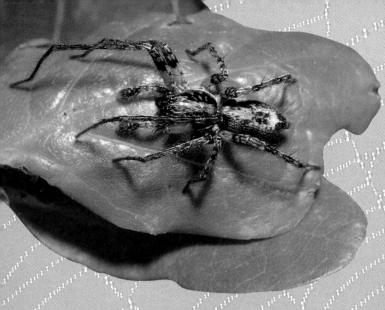

Focus on

Female spiders attract males by giving off a special scent called a pheromone. Each species has a different pheromone, to help the males find the right mate. Once he has found a female, the male has to give off the right signals so that the female realizes he is not a meal. Courtship signals include special dances, drumming, buzzing, or plucking the female's web in a particular way. Some males distract the females with a gift of food while others tie up the females with strands of silk before mating.

NOISY COURTSHIP

The male buzzing spider (*Anyphaena accentuata*) beats his abdomen against a leaf to attract a mate. The sound is loud enough for people to hear. He often buzzes on the roof of the female's oak-leaf nest. Other male hunting spiders make courtship sounds by rubbing one part of their bodies against another.

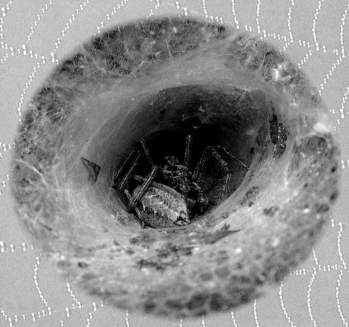

MATING SUCCESS

The male grass funnel-weaver (*Agelena labyrinthica*) is almost as large as the female and can be quite aggressive. He taps his palps on her funnel web to announce his arrival. If the female is ready to mate, she draws in her legs and collapses as if she is paralysed.

The male presents a gift to the female.

BEARING GIFTS

A male nursery-web spider (*Pisaura mirabilis*) presents an insect gift to the female. He has neatly gift-wrapped his present in a dense covering of very shiny white silk. Once the female has accepted his gift and is feeding, the male can mate with her in safety.

Courtship

COURTSHIP DANCES

Spiders that can see well at a distance often dance together before mating. This wolf spider (*Lycosa*) waves his palps like semaphore flags to a female in the distance. Male spiders also strike special poses and use their long, stout front legs to make signalling more effective.

A RISKY BUSINESS

Male garden spiders (*Araneus*) often have great difficulty courting a female. They are usually much smaller and lighter than the female and have to persuade her to move on to a special mating thread. The male joins the mating thread to the edge of the female's web. He tweaks the silk strands of her web to lure the female towards him.

COURTSHIP PROBLEMS

This male green orb-weaver (*Araniella cucurbitina*) has lost four legs in the courtship process. When the female attacked him, he swung down on a silken dragline. He will climb back up again when it is safe.

JUMPING SPIDERS

This pair of jumping spiders (*Salticus*) are ready to mate. Male jumping spiders impress females by twirling and waltzing, waving their legs, palps and abdomens. Females often attract more than one male and they have to compete to mate with her. The female reaches out and touches the male when she is ready to mate.

Spider Eggs

Female spiders usually lay their eggs a week or two after mating, although some spiders wait several months. Not all the eggs are laid at once and many spiders lay several batches, usually at night when it is safer. The female may lay from one to over 1,000 eggs per batch. Most spiders lay their eggs on a circle of silk together with some of the male's stored sperm. It is not until now that the eggs are fertilized. The outer layer of the eggs gradually hardens and the female spins a cocoon around them for extra protection.

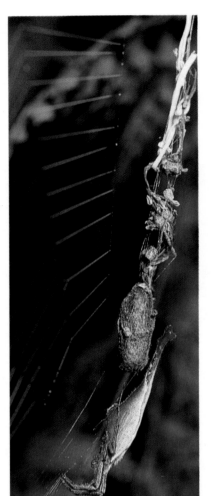

Ananse the Spider Man

A hero of many folk tales in West Africa and the Caribbean is Ananse. He is both a spider and a man. When things are going well he is a man, but in times of danger he becomes a  *spider. Ananse likes to trick the other animals and get the better of those who are much bigger than himself. He may be greedy and selfish, but he is also funny. He is a hero because he brought the gift of telling stories to people.*

◀ **IN DISGUISE**
To hide their eggs from hungry predators, spiders may camouflage the cocoons with plant material, insect bodies, mud or sand. This scorpion spider (*Arachnura*) hangs her brown egg cases from her web like a string of rubbish, then poses as a dead leaf beneath them. Other spiders hide egg cases under stones or bark, or fix leaves together like a purse.

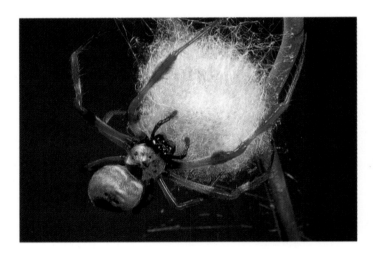

▲ **SPINNING THE COCOON**
A *Nephila edulis* spins her egg cocoon. She uses special strong, loopy silk that traps a lot of air and helps to stop the eggs drying out. Her eggs are covered with a sticky coating to fix them to the silk. The final protective blanket of yellow silk will turn green, camouflaging the cocoon.

◄ FLIMSY EGG CASE

The daddy-longlegs spider (*Pholcus*) uses hardly any silk for her egg case. Just a few strands hold the eggs loosely together. Producing a large egg case uses up a lot of energy and females with large egg cases often have shrunken bodies. The daddy-longlegs carries the eggs around in her jaws. She is unable to feed until the eggs hatch.

SILK NEST ►

The woodlouse spider (*Dysdera crocota*) lays her eggs in a silken cell under the ground. She also lives in this shelter, where she is safer from enemies. At night, the woodlouse spider emerges from its silken house to look for woodlice, which it kills with its enormous fangs.

◄ CAREFUL MOTHER

A green lynx spider (*Peucetia*) protects her egg case on a cactus. She fixes the case with silk lines, like a tent's guy ropes, and drives off any enemies. If necessary, she cuts the silk lines and lets the egg case swing in mid-air, balancing on top like a trapeze artist. If she has to move her eggs to a safer place, she drags the case behind her with silk threads.

GUARD DUTY ►

Many female spiders carry their eggs around with them. This rusty wandering spider (*Cupiennius getazi*) carries her egg sac attached to her spinnerets. Spiders that do this often moisten the eggs in water and sunbathe to warm them and so speed up their development.

Did you know? A female garden spider can lay over 1,000 eggs in under 10 minutes.

Spiderlings

Most spider **eggs** hatch within a few days or weeks of being laid. The spiderlings (baby spiders) do not usually have any hairs, spines, claws or colour when they first hatch. They feed on the **egg** yolk stored in their bodies and grow fast. They cast off their first skin in a process called **moulting**. Spiderlings have to moult several times as they grow into adults. After the first moult, young spiders look like tiny versions of their parents. Most baby spiders look after themselves from the moment of hatching, but some mothers guard and feed their young until they leave the nest. Male spiders do not look after their young at all.

▲ HATCHING OUT

These spiderlings are emerging from their egg case. Spiderlings may stay inside the case for some time after hatching. Some spiders have an egg tooth to help break them out of the egg, but mother spiders may also help their young to hatch. Spiderlings from very different species look similar.

◀ NURSERY WEB

Female nursery-web spiders (*Pisaura mirabilis*) build a silk tent for their egg cases when they are ready to hatch. The mother sits on the tent and guards the eggs and hatchlings for a week or so. The baby spiders moult once and then gradually leave the nest to start life on their own.

Nursery-web spider guarding her nest

Nursery tent

Egg case

▲ A SPIDER BALL

Garden spiderlings (*Araneus*) stay together for several days after hatching. They form small gold and black balls that break apart if danger threatens, but re-form when danger has passed.

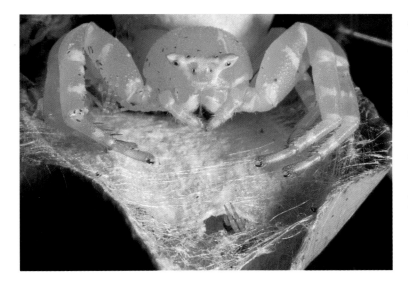

◄ BABY BODIES

A female crab spider watches over her young as they hatch out. Spider eggs contain a lot of yolk, which provides a good supply of energy for the baby spiders. They are well developed when they hatch out, with the same body shape and number of legs as adults. Baby spiders, however, cannot produce silk or venom until their first moult.

Spiderlings cling to special hairs on their mother's back for about a week.

BABY CARRIER ▶

Pardosa wolf spiders carry their egg cases joined to their spinnerets. When the eggs are ready to hatch, the mother tears open the case and the babies climb on to her back. If the spiderlings fall off, they can find their way back by following silk lines the mother trails behind her.

Spotted wolf spider (*Pardosa amentata*)

The mother spider feeds on a fly.

Silk threads are called gossamer.

Did you know?
Many young spiders often feed on their own mother's body.

▲ FOOD FROM MUM

The mothercare spider (*Theridion sisyphium*) feeds her young on food brought up from her stomach. The rich soup is made of digested insects and cells lining her gut. The babies shake her legs to beg for food. They grow faster than babies that feed themselves.

▲ BALLOON FLIGHT

Many spiderlings take to the air to find new places to live or to avoid being eaten by their brothers and sisters. On a warm day with light winds, they float through the air on strands of silk drawn out from their spinnerets. This is called ballooning.

Moulting

Spiders do not grow gradually, like we do. Instead they grow in a series of steps. At each step, the spider grows a new outer skin, or exoskeleton, under the old one and moults (sheds) the old one. Lost or damaged legs and other body parts can be replaced during a moult. Small spiders moult in a few hours, but larger spiders may need several days. A young spider moults about five to ten times as it grows into an adult. A few spiders continue to moult throughout their adult lives.

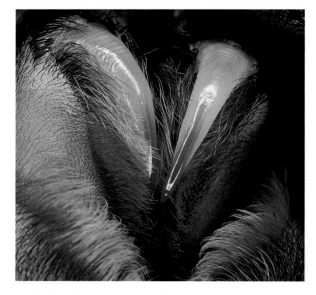

▲ **COLOUR CHANGE**
Adult spiders that have just moulted are quite pale for a while and do not show their true colours for a day or so. The fangs of this newly moulted tarantula have no colour as yet.

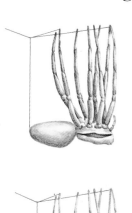

1 The first split forms along the carapace.

2 The split moves back along the abdomen.

3 Carefully the spider heaves its body out of the old skin.

4 The spider expands its body to stretch the new skeleton.

▲ **STAGES IN MOULTING**
The main stages in the moulting process of a spider are shown above. It is a dangerous process. Legs can get broken and spiders are vulnerable to enemies as they moult since they cannot defend themselves or run away.

▲ **THE OLD SKIN**
This is the old exoskeleton of a fishing spider (*Dolomedes*). The piece at the top is the lid of the carapace. The holes are where the legs fitted inside the skin.

HOW MANY MOULTS? ▶

This young red and white spider (*Enoplognatha ovata*) is in the middle of moulting. It is hiding under a leaf out of sight of enemies. A larger adult spider seems to have come to investigate. It is not until the final moult that a spider takes on its adult colours. Most spiders stop moulting when they become adults. Smaller species need fewer moults to reach adult size. Males also go through fewer moults than females because they are smaller when fully grown.

◀ MOULTING PROCESS

A tarantula pulls itself free of its old skin. Before a spider moults, it stops feeding and rests for a while. During this time, a new wrinkled exoskeleton forms underneath the old one and part of the old skin is absorbed back into the body to be recycled. The spider then pumps blood into the front of its body, making it swell and split the old skin, which is now very thin.

Did you know? Spiders can grow new palps, fangs and spinnerets when they moult.

A NEW SKIN ▶

This Chilean rose tarantula (*Grammostola cala*) moulted recently. Its new skin is bright and colourful. It looks very hairy because new hairs have replaced those that have been lost or damaged. When a spider first escapes from its old skin, it flexes its legs to make sure the joints stay supple. As the new skeleton dries out, it hardens. The skin on the abdomen stays fairly stretchy, so it can expand as the spider eats, or fill with eggs in females.

51

Spiders Everywhere

From mountain tops, caves and deserts to forests, marshes and grasslands, there are few places on Earth without spiders. Even remote islands are inhabited by spiders, perhaps blown there on the wind or carried on floating logs. Many spiders are quite at home in our houses and some travel the world on cargo ships. Many spiders live on sewage works, where there are plenty of flies for them to feed on. Spiders are not very common in watery places, however, since they cannot breathe underwater. There are also no spiders in Antarctica, although they do manage to live on the edge of the Arctic. To survive the winter in cool places, spiders may stay as eggs, hide away under grass, rocks or bark or make nests together. Some even have a type of antifreeze to stop their bodies freezing up.

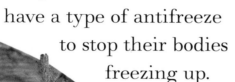

▲ **HEDGEROW WEBS**
One of the most common spiders on bushes and hedges in Europe and Asia is the hammock web (*Linyphia triangularis*). One hedge may contain thousands of webs with their haphazard threads.

Did you know? Some spiders live in the web of another species and steal its food.

◄ **SPIDER IN THE SINK**
The spiders that people sometimes find in the sink or the bath are usually male house spiders (*Tegenaria*) that have fallen in while searching for a mate. They cannot climb back up the smooth sides because they do not have gripping tufts of hair on their feet like hunting spiders.

▲ CAVE SPIDER

The cave orb-weaver (*Meta menardi*) almost always builds its web in very dark places, often suspended from the roof. It is found in caves, mines, hollow trees, railway tunnels, drains, wells and the corners of outbuildings in Europe, Asia and North America.

▲ DESERT SPIDER

The main problem for desert spiders such as this white lady (*Leucorhestris arenicola*) is the lack of water. It hides away from the intense heat in a burrow beneath the sand and, in times of drought, may go into suspended animation. Desert spiders live in different places to avoid competition for food.

◀ SEASHORE SPIDER

This beach wolf spider (*Arctosa littoralis*) is well camouflaged on the sand. It lives in a very hostile place. Waves pound on the beach and shift the sand, there is little fresh water and the sun quickly dries everything out. There is little food, although insects gather on seaweed, rocks and plants growing along the edge of the shore.

RAINFOREST SPIDER ▶

The greatest variety of spiders is to be found in the rainforests of the tropics. Here the climate is warm all year round and plenty of food is always available. This forest huntsman (*Pandercetes plumipes*) is well camouflaged against a tree trunk covered in lichen. To hide, it presses its body close against the tree. It lives in Malaysia where it is found in gardens as well as the rainforest.

Focus on

No spiders live in the open sea, but several hunt in and around fresh water. If they sense danger, they dive down underwater by holding on to plants. Only one spider, the water spider (*Argyroneta aquatica*), spends its whole life underwater. It lives in ponds, lakes and slow-moving streams in Europe and Asia. It still needs to breathe oxygen from the air, so it lives in a bubble of air called a diving bell. It does not need a regular supply of food because its body works very slowly. It catches prey by sticking its legs out of the diving bell to pick up vibrations in the water.

FOOD FROM THE WATER

This fishing spider (*Dolomedes fimbriatus*) has caught a colourful reed-frog. Fishing spiders also eat tadpoles, small fish and insects that have fallen into the water. Their venom paralyses their prey very quickly, so it has little chance of escape.

FISHING FOR FOOD

Fishing spiders sit on floating leaves or twigs with their front legs resting on the surface of the water. Hairs on their legs detect ripples. The spider can work out the position of prey from the direction and distance between the ripples. Ripples from twigs or leaves falling into the water often confuse the spider.

Water Spiders

DINING TABLE

Neither water spiders nor fishing spiders can eat in the water, because it would dilute their digestive chemicals. Water spiders feed inside their diving bells, while fishing spiders have their meals on the bank or an object floating in the water. This fishing spider is eating a stickleback on a mossy bank. The tail of the fish is caught in the sticky tentacles of a sundew plant.

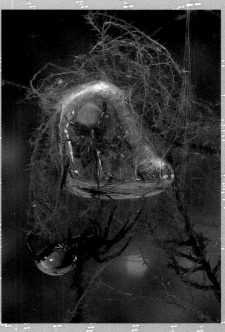

1 To make a diving bell, the water spider spins a web fixed to an underwater plant. Then it swims to the surface to trap a bubble of air, which it carries down to the web.

2 The spider releases the bubble, which floats up to be trapped inside the roof of the web. To fill the diving bell with air takes up to six trips to and from the surface.

3 Once the bell is finished, the spider eats, mates and lays its eggs inside. This male spider is visiting a female. She will only leave her bell to collect more air or catch food

Spider Families

To help them study spiders, scientists divide the 35,000 known species into three groups, known as suborders. The three groups are: araneomorphs (true spiders), mygalomorphs (tarantulas, purse-web spiders and trapdoor spiders) and the rare liphistiomorphs (giant trapdoor spiders). Most spiders are araneomorphs with jaws that close together sideways. These groups are further divided into 105 families. Spiders are put in families according to such things as the arrangement of their eyes, their silk-making glands or the number of claws on their feet. Some of the larger families, as well as the rarest, are shown here.

Giant trapdoor spider
(*Liphistius desultor*)

▲ **GIANT TRAPDOOR SPIDERS**
The Liphistiomorphs are rare spiders that live in Southeast Asia and Japan. There are about 20 different species. They live in burrows with trapdoor entrances. These very primitive spiders have bands across their abdomens and may look more like spiders that lived millions of years ago.

Money spider
(*Linyphia montana*)

▲ **MONEY SPIDERS**
The Linyphiidae family are the second largest spider family with about 3,700 species. Linyphiids are usually very small and are commonly called money spiders. They are by far the commonest spiders in cooler, temperate parts of the world. They build hammock webs and hang upside-down beneath them.

▲ **ORB-WEB SPIDERS**
The main family of orb-weavers is the Araneidae with about 2,600 species. A typical member is this Jamaican orb-weaver (*Argiope*). It has a stout body with a rounded abdomen and sits in the centre of its circular web. Garden spiders belong to this family.

HUNTSMAN SPIDERS ▶

The Sparassidae (also called Heteropodidae) huntsman spiders are a family of about 1,000 species. Most live in tropical regions where they are sometimes called giant crab spiders. The Australian huntsman is one of the largest members with a body length of over 30mm. Some species of this family have been discovered in crates of bananas.

Australian Huntsman
(Isopeda)

Classification Chart

Kingdom	**Animalia**	(all animals)
Phylum	**Arthropoda**	(animals with exoskeletons and jointed legs)
Class	**Arachnida**	(arthropods with eight legs)
Order	**Araneae**	(spiders)
Suborder	**Araneomorphae**	(true spiders)
Family	**Theridiidae**	(comb-footed spiders)
Genus	***Latrodectus***	(widow spiders)
Species	***Mactans***	(black widow spider)

◀ SPIDER NAMES

Scientists classify (group) every spider and give it a Latin name. This chart shows how the black widow spider is classified. Few spiders have common names and these vary from country to country. Their Latin name, however, stays the same all over the world.

Black spotted jumper
(Acragus)

Did you know? The first spiders lived about 400 million years ago on Earth.

◀ JUMPING SPIDERS

The world's largest spider family is the Salticidae containing over 4,000 species of jumping spiders. These small, active daylight hunters have large front eyes and an amazing ability to stalk and jump on prey. They mostly live in tropical areas and many are brightly coloured.

▲ CRAB SPIDERS

Another very large family is the Thomisidae with about 3,000 species of crab spiders. Crab spiders are found all over the world. They do not usually build webs and many sit waiting on flowers or leaves to ambush prey. They often rely on good camouflage to blend in with their surroundings and avoid predators.

Spider Relatives

Spiders belong to a large group of animals called arthropods (the word means jointed foot). Other arthropods include crabs, prawns, woodlice, centipedes and insects. Spiders are members of the group of arthropods that have eight legs, called arachnids. Other arachnids include scorpions, mites, ticks and harvestmen. Spiders are different from other arachnids because they have silk glands in the abdomen. Mites produce silk from the mouth and pseudoscorpions from the jaws. Spiders are also the only arachnids to inject venom with fangs. Scorpions have a stinging tail and pseudoscorpions have venom in their palps.

▲ **CAMEL SPIDER**
This scorpion is fighting a camel spider. People once thought camel spiders could kill camels, but they are not even poisonous. They have big, powerful jaws and are fast runners. They usually live in dry places feeding on insects. Camel spiders are also called sun spiders, even though they are not spiders.

Scorpions use their large pincers to grab, crush and tear prey, which is then passed to the jaws.

The sting is used to subdue prey and in self-defence.

The exoskeleton is like tough leathery armour.

Fine bristles on the legs are sensitive to vibrations.

◀ **SCORPION**
Scorpions are much larger than most spiders. They have two large pincer-like palps at the front and a narrow tail with a poisonous sting at the rear. Some scorpions can kill people, though they sting mainly in self-defence. Young scorpions are born alive and are carried on their mother's back for two to four weeks.

▲ WHIP SPIDER

The closest relatives of spiders may be the whip spiders, such as this *Damon variegatus*. The first pair of legs are very long, like whips. They are used for sensing prey at a distance, not for walking. Unlike spiders, whip spiders have an abdomen divided into segments and palps like pincers for grabbing their prey. They hunt at night, but are not poisonous.

▲ VELVET MITE

These tiny spider relatives do not have bodies divided into two parts, like spiders. Many feed on plants and are serious pests. Other mites are parasites, feeding off much larger animals.

Did you know? Some scorpions have special light-sensitive cells in their tails.

▲ SEA SPIDER

In spite of their name, sea spiders are not spiders at all. They used to be grouped with the arachnids, but are now put in a separate class of their own and are probably not closely related. Sea spiders have a tiny body with four, five or six pairs of long, spindly legs. Some live in the freezing waters off the coast of Antarctica. This one is from Tasmania.

HARVESTMAN ▲

Often called harvest spiders, these long-legged arachnids are common around harvest time. They use their long legs to detect and trap insects, since they have no poison or silk glands.
The body of a harvestman is in one piece and it has only two eyes on a turret near the middle of the body. To protect itself from predators, a harvestman gives off a nasty smell.

59

Spiders and People

Most people are scared of spiders. With their long legs, hairy bodies and a habit of lurking in dark corners, spiders have not made themselves popular. Yet they are truly fascinating animals. Only a handful are dangerous to people and medicines, called antivenins, can now help people recover quickly from a deadly spider's bite. Many spiders are useful in helping to control insect pests not only on crops and in gardens, but also in our homes. In most countries it is bad luck to kill a spider, but people are their greatest threat. We destroy their habitats and reduce their numbers in the wild by collecting spiders to be sold as pets.

▲ FEAR OF SPIDERS

This man is obviously unafraid of spiders. He is quite happy to have a tarantula walk over his face. Some experts think that we are born with a fear of spiders. This may be because a few spiders were dangerous to our ancestors in the distant past when we lived closer to nature.

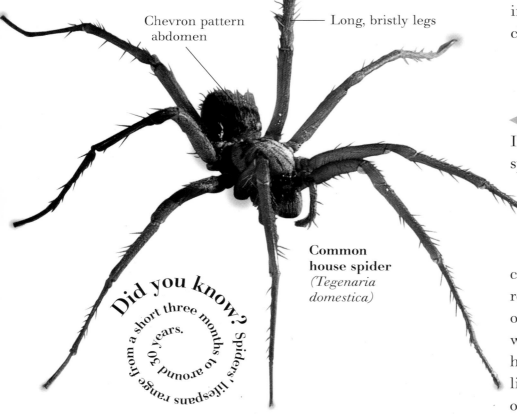

Chevron pattern abdomen

Long, bristly legs

Common house spider
(*Tegenaria domestica*)

Did you know? Spiders' lifespans range from a short three months to around 30 years.

◄ HOUSE SPIDERS

In cooler, temperate countries, house spiders (*Tegenaria*) are some of the commonest spiders. The common house spider leaves unwelcome, dusty sheet webs, called cobwebs, in the corners of rooms and against windows. A maze of trip wires over the surface of the web traps earwigs, flies and other household pests. House spiders may live for several years in the shelter of our homes.

◀ HABITATS IN DANGER

People destroy and pollute the places in which spiders and many other animals live. Clearing tropical rainforests, such as this one in Paraguay, South America, is particularly destructive. A huge variety of species of spiders live in the rainforest, many of them not yet known to scientists.

Little Miss Muffett
Miss Muffett was the daughter of the Reverend Thomas Muffett, a spider expert. When she was ill, her father made her eat crushed spiders as a cure. This made her terrified of spiders. A fear of spiders is called arachnophobia.

◀ SPIDERS IN MEDICINE

This Piaroa shaman (medicine man) from Venezuela, South America, uses a tarantula hunting mask as part of a ceremony. In Europe and America, spiders have been used in the past to treat malaria, plague, toothache and headache. Sometimes the spiders were hung in a bag around the neck or eaten.

Ladybird spider
(Eresus niger)

RARE SPIDERS ▶

Fewer than 20 species of spiders around the world are listed as threatened with extinction. They include the ladybird spider shown here. There must be, however, hundreds or even thousands more spiders in danger that we do not know about yet. Spiders need our protection. For example, the Mexican red-knee tarantula (*Brachypelma smithi*) is now rare in the wild because of over-collection by the pet trade. Spiders that have been bred in captivity may help this species to survive.

GLOSSARY

abdomen
The rear part of a spider's body.

ambush
To hide and wait, and then make a surprise attack.

antennae
A pair of feelers on an insect's head, used mainly for smelling, but also for feeling things.

arachnid
One of a group of small meat-eating animals with eight legs, such as spiders, mites, ticks and scorpions.

Araneidae
The family of spiders that usually build orb webs.

araneomorph
A typical or true spider with jaws that close together sideways.

arthropod
An animal without a backbone that has many jointed legs and an exoskeleton on the outside of its body. Arthropods include spiders, insects, crabs and woodlice.

ballooning
Floating away on strands of silk blown by the wind.

book lung
An organ in a spider's body that takes oxygen from the air. Most spiders have one pair of book lungs in the abdomen. Inside is an air-filled cavity filled with thin flaps (like the pages of a book). Blood flowing through the flaps takes in oxygen.

camouflage
Colours, patterns or shapes that allow a spider to blend in perfectly with its surroundings.

carapace
The shell-like covering over the front part of a spider's body, the cephalothorax.

cephalothorax
The front part of a spider's body, to which the legs are attached.

chelicerae
The jaws of a spider. Each jaw has two parts – a large basal segment and a fang.

classification
Arranging animals according to their similarities and differences in order to study them and suggest how they may be related.

cocoon
A silky covering or egg case made to protect a spider's eggs.

crab spiders
Ambushing spiders in the family Thomisidae that do not usually build webs and are often shaped rather like crabs.

cribellum
A plate through which a special kind of fine, woolly silk is produced in a group of spiders known as the cribellates (lace-web weavers). The plate is just in front of the spinnerets at the back of the abdomen.

daddy-longlegs spiders
Spiders in the family Pholcidae. They have very long legs and build untidy webs under stones, in caves or the corners of rooms.

digestion
The process by which food is broken down so it can be taken into the body.

dragline
The line of silk on which a spider drops down, often to escape danger, and then climbs back up.

embolus
A structure at the end of a male spider's palp that is used to transfer sperm to the female.

exoskeleton
The hard outer skin or shell that covers a spider's body.

fang
The piercing part of a spider's jaw. Poison comes out of a hole at the tip of the fang.

fertilization
The joining together of a male sperm and a female egg to start a new life.

head
The part of a spider that carries the eyes. It is separated from the spider's chest by a shallow groove.

hub
The central circle of an orb web.

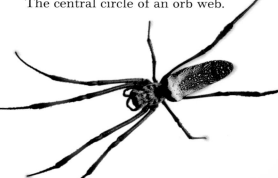

insect
A small animal with a body that is divided into three parts, with six legs and usually one or two pairs of wings.

jumping spiders
Spiders in the family Salticidae that are curious, daytime hunters with two stout front pairs of legs. Many are brightly coloured.

lynx spiders
Spiders in the family Oxyopidae that hunt on plants. They have pointed abdomens, spiny legs and fairly large eyes. Females fix their egg cases to plants and guard them until they hatch.

lyriform organ
A sensory organ, especially on the legs, that picks up vibrations.

maxillae
A pair of secondary jaws that help to break up food.

mimicry
When a spider copies the shape of another animal or an object such as a bird dropping or stick. Spiders use mimicry to hide from enemies and prey.

moulting
The process by which a spider sheds its skin.

mygalomorph
A more primitive spider with jaws that strike downward. Mygalomorphs have two pairs of book lungs and no tracheae (breathing tubes). Most species are large, hairy and live in burrows, such as trapdoor spiders and tarantulas.

nursery-web spiders
Females in the family Pisauridae that carry their egg cases around with them in their jaws and make a silk tent when the eggs are ready to hatch.

palp (pedipalp)
Short, leg-like feeler either side of the mouthparts. In the adult male, the end segment is modified for putting sperm into the female.

paralyse
To make an animal powerless and unable to move, although it is still alive.

pheromone
A chemical scent produced by spiders to attract members of the opposite sex and, in some spiders, to attract prey.

predator
An animal that catches and kills other animals for food.

prey
An animal that is hunted by other animals for their food.

recluse spiders
Spiders in the family Loxoscelidae that are very poisonous to people and often spin webs in buildings.

scopula
A dense brush of hairs on the feet of some spiders that helps them to grip smooth surfaces.

spiderling
A young spider that looks more or less like the fully-grown adult, but is smaller.

spinneret
An opening at the end of a spider's abdomen through which silk is pulled out.

spitting spiders
Spiders in the family Scytodidae with a domed carapace and large venom glands that produce glue as well as venom.

stabilimentum
A special band of white silk, usually a zigzag, placed across the centre of the web of some spiders.

tarantula
One of the giant, hairy spiders belonging to the family Theraphosidae. In Australia, it is often the name given to the huntsman spiders. The true tarantula is a wolf spider from the genus *Lycosa* found in southern Europe.

trachea (plural tracheae)
Fine tubes through which air is carried around the spider's body. They open to the outside through holes called spiracles.

trichobothrium (plural trichobothria)
A long, fine hair on a spider's leg that detects air vibrations and currents. Sometimes called a touch-at-a-distance receptor.

Uloboridae
Mainly tropical and sub-tropical, feather-legged spiders that are the only spiders not to have venom. They build orb webs and have a cribellum to spin silk. Some uloborids build communal webs and live together.

venom
Poisonous fluid produced by nearly all spiders that is used to kill their prey.

wolf spiders
Members of the family Lycosidae. They are hunters with fairly large eyes and live mostly on the ground. Females carry their egg cases attached to their spinnerets.

INDEX

A

abdomen 4, 20, 34, 43, 51
Agroeca 16
angling spider 24–5
arachnids 5, 62
arachnophobia 60–1
araneomorphs 56, 62
arthropods 58–9, 62
Augusta glyphica 39

B

baboon spiders 8–9
bird dropping disguise 39
bird-eating spiders 7–9,
    26–7
bites 8–9, 17, 32–3
black widow spider 33, 42
blood 10–13
book lung 11, 62
bolas spider 24–5
brain 10–11
breathing 11–12
burrows 9, 30–1, 34, 36
buzzing spider 44

C

camel spider 58
camouflage 6–7, 21, 30–1,
    36, 38–40, 43, 46, 57
cannibalism 27, 29, 42
carapace 4, 50, 62
cave spiders 14, 53
cephalothorax 4, 62
chelicerae 4, 11, 62
chitin 10
climbing 9, 12–13, 52
cobwebs 60
cocoons 16, 43, 46–7, 62
colour 5–6, 36–9, 40,
    42–3, 50
comb-footed spiders 6, 23

D

communal webs 22–3
courtship 28, 44–5
crab spiders 6, 33, 38, 40–1,
    49, 57, 62
cribellate spiders 17, 20, 62

daddy-longlegs spider 25,
    47, 62
defence 9, 36–7
digestive system 10–11,
    34, 41, 55
displays 28, 36
dome weavers 23
draglines 12, 45, 62

E

eggs 8, 16, 25, 34, 42–3,
    46–9
exoskeleton 4, 10, 50–1, 62
eyes 9–10, 14–15, 24, 28

F

fangs 4, 9, 11, 25, 30–5,
    41, 50, 62
feet 9–10, 12–13, 29, 34
fishing spiders 12, 27, 54–5
flower spiders 6, 40–1
food 4, 9, 26–7, 34–5, 41
funnel-web spiders 22, 31

G

garden spiders 12, 18–19,
    34, 42, 45, 48, 56
golden wheel spider 36
gossamer 49
grass funnel-weaver 44

H

habitats 52–3, 61
hairs 7–10, 12–14, 29,
    49, 51
hammock webs 22, 52, 56
harvestman 58–9
hearing 10, 34
heather spider 40
house spiders 52, 60
hunting spiders 12, 15,
    26–9, 32
huntsman spiders 10, 15,
    39, 53, 57

J

jumping spiders 13–15,
    26–9, 38, 45, 57, 63

K

kite spider 6

L

lace-weaver 17
ladybird spider 43, 61
legs 4, 10, 12–13, 28, 50–1
lichen huntsman spider 39
liphistiomorphs 56
lobed argiope spider 35
lynx spiders 15, 27, 47, 63
lyriform organs 10, 34, 63

M

malmignatte spider 32
mating 42–3
maxillae 34, 63
mimicry 38, 63
mites 58–9
money spiders 15, 23, 56
mothercare spider 49
moulting 10, 50–1, 63
mouth 10–11, 34
movement 12–13
mygalomorphs 7, 35, 56, 63

N

Nephila 5, 7, 21, 43, 46
nerves 10
nests 16, 44
net-casting spider 24–5
nursery-web spiders 44, 48,
    63

O

ocelli 14–15
ogre-faced spider 24
orb-web spiders 7, 10, 15,
    17–21, 26, 45, 56

P

palps 4, 10, 42, 63
pheromones 44, 63
poison 11, 17, 25, 32–5, 40
predators 36–7
prey 5, 9–12, 17, 19–21
    24–35
pseudoscorpions 58
purse-web spider 30, 56

R

raft spider 12
recluse spiders 32, 63
red and white spider 51
reproduction 11, 42–9

S

scaffold
    webs 22–5
scopulae 13, 29, 63
scorpions 58
scorpion spider 46
sea spider 59
senses 5, 10, 14–15
sheet webs 22–3
silk 4, 10–11, 16–25,
    30, 35, 42, 44
smell, sense of 10, 14, 44
social spiders 22–3
Sosippus mimus 43
spear-jawed spider 38
spiderlings 48–9, 63
spinnerets 4, 16–17, 47, 49
spinning 4–5, 10, 12, 16–25
spitting spiders 24–5, 63
stomach 11, 34
sun spiders 58
swamp spider 12

T

tarantulas 6–9, 22, 27,
    32–3, 35, 50–1, 60–61, 63
taste, sense of 10
ticks 58
touch, sense of 5, 10, 14–15
    19, 21, 27, 31
trachea 11, 63
trapdoor spiders 13, 15, 22,
    26, 30–1, 35–6, 56
triangular spider 5
trichobothria 10, 63
trip wires 30–1
tube-web spiders 16, 30–1

V

venom 32–5, 63
violin spider 32

W

wandering spiders 32, 34, 47
warning displays and
    colours 36–9, 41
water spider 54–5
webs 4–5, 10, 12, 15–23
whip spider 59
white lady spider 53
widow spiders 6, 32–3, 42
wolf spiders 7–8, 15, 31–2,
    38, 45, 49, 53, 63
woodlouse spider 15, 47